THE CRAFT
AND MAKING OF
DOPE THIEF

A THRILLING GUIDE TO SEASON ONE
AND THE FUTURE OF THE SERIES

MICHAEL S. SAGE

1

The Craft and Making of Dope Thief

A Thrilling Guide to Season One and the Future of the Series

By

Michael S. Sage

Copyright© Michael S. Sage,2025

<u>Disclaimer</u>

This book is an independent publication and is not authorized, licensed, or endorsed by Apple TV+, the creators, producers, or distributors of *Dope Thief*. All names, trademarks, and copyrights related to *Dope Thief* remain the property of their respective owners.

The author and publisher of this guide are independent and have created this work solely for the purpose of commentary, analysis, and educational discussion. This book offers unofficial coverage of *Dope Thief* and is intended for fans who wish to explore the themes, production, and cultural impact of the series in greater depth.

Limitation of Liability

The author and publisher have made every effort to ensure the accuracy and completeness of the information contained in this book. However, they make no representations or warranties regarding the applicability, fitness, or completeness of the content for any purpose.

By reading this book, you agree that under no circumstances shall the author or publisher be held liable for any direct, indirect, incidental, consequential, or special damages arising from the use of, or reliance on, the information provided herein. This includes but is not limited to

4

Gratitude

Creating this book has been a journey fueled by passion, curiosity, and countless hours of dedication. I want to extend my deepest thanks to the readers who continue to support independent publishing and celebrate in-depth explorations of the shows and stories we love. To the creative minds behind *Dope Thief*, your work inspired this deep dive, and your artistry has left a lasting impression.

To friends, family, and fellow fans—thank you for your encouragement, insights, and unwavering belief in this project. Your support means everything. Most importantly, thank you, the reader, for choosing this book. Your interest and engagement breathe life into every word written. Stay curious, stay inspired, and never stop exploring the stories that move you.

Table Of Contents

INTRODUCTION

A Dive Into Crime and Consequence: Why Dope Thief Captivates Viewers

Dope Thief emerges as a spine-tingling examination of deceit, consequence, and survival in the crowded field of crime dramas, rather than merely being another grim story about criminals and lawmen. Based on Dennis Tafoya's 2009 novel, *Dope Thief* was created by Peter Craig and debuted on Apple TV+ on March 14, 2025. Its rich characters, dramatic environment, and biting indictment of desperate decisions made in a fragmented world immediately captivated viewers.

The idea is surprisingly straightforward: two Philadelphia-based boyhood friends, Manny Carvalho (Wagner Moura) and Ray Driscoll (Brian Tyree Henry), rob drug dealers by posing as DEA agents. Their initial strategy is low risk, high reward—a means of taking advantage of the criminal underworld they are all too familiar with. Targeting a drug operation that is being watched by actual DEA agents, however, throws their plan into a dangerous whirlpool of federal attention and cartel retaliation. It's a typical example of hubris colliding with reality, as anarchy swiftly replaces the appearance of control.

Dope Thief presents itself as a thriller based on moral ambiguity and unpredictability from the first scene, which is a stressful raid on a Philadelphia row house that concludes with the terrifying discovery that Ray and Manny are imposters. The high-stakes intensity of the pilot, which was directed by Ridley Scott, establishes the tone for the eight-episode series. This suspense is maintained by other directors, such as Jonathan van Tulleken (Shōgun) and Marcela Said (Narcos: Mexico), who provide action-packed scenes of shootouts, pursuits, and betrayals, all supported by Apple TV+'s renownedly high production value.

Dope Thief is more than just action, though. Character analysis is intense, particularly when viewed from Ray Driscoll's perspective. Ray's understanding of "the game" offers him an advantage as a recovering addict and former dealer, but it also makes him a prime target. Ray's growing desperation is viscerally embodied by Henry, in his first executive producer role. At first, his confidence and swagger enable him to bluff his way through risky situations, but as things go out of control, we can see the weaknesses in his façade. As Ray deals with threats from the DEA, violent gangs, and an enigmatic, vindictive individual who can only be identified by a frightening Boston-accented voice via a recovered walkie-talkie, Henry's portrayal is both captivating and eerie.

As Manny, whose hopes of a secure life with his lover Sherry are dashed by the pair's error, Wagner Moura is just as captivating. The narrative is emotionally anchored by their friendship, which has been strengthened by a shared past and put to the test by their unraveling future. Another level of depth is introduced by Marin Ireland's portrayal of Mina, a DEA agent injured after a failed robbery. In addition to being professional, her pursuit of Ray and Manny is also personal, laced with hurt and repressed rage.

The stakes are raised by the supporting cast, which includes Kate Mulgrew as Theresa, Ray's feisty stepmother, and Ving Rhames as Ray's imprisoned father Bart. Mulgrew in particular, who frequently acts as Ray's sane voice in the midst of his collapsing world, adds scathing humor and emotional weight to the narrative. Rare but welcome comic relief is provided by her witty one-liners, such as the memorable "YOU DIDN'T GIVE TO THE POOR!" when Ray tries to defend his actions.

There are issues with *Dope Thief*. Sometimes, flashbacks to Ray's past—such as the passing of his fiancée Marietta—feel like filler, extending a plot that could have worked well as a feature film into a full-length television series. There is no spark or need for the romantic subplot between Ray and Michelle, Bart's lawyer. However, these errors pale in comparison to the total influence of the series.

Dope Thief has received largely positive reviews from critics, with a Metacritic score of 74 and an 86% approval rating on Rotten Tomatoes. Many reviews commend the series' impressive performances and fast pacing, while others point out its derivative qualities. The program may seem similar, but its execution makes it a "riveting ride," as The A.V. Club pointed out in its B-grade review.

Dope Thief's vivid sense of place is what makes it unique. The show, which is set and produced in Philadelphia, incorporates local textures to anchor the story in a concrete reality, such as Eagles memorabilia and Pennsylvania Dutch conversation. It feels both local and universal because of its uniqueness, which also places it in line with other crime dramas set in Philadelphia, such as Mare of Easttown. Furthermore, Peter Craig creates a sense of lingering disquiet by placing the scenario in the post-COVID age, complete with surgical masks and supply chain disruptions. It's a subdued yet powerful way to portray a world where dread and uncertainty are ubiquitous, particularly for those on the periphery of society.

In the end, *Dope Thief* captivates viewers by appealing to their basic anxieties: the fear of being discovered, the regret of previous transgressions, and the unachievable want to avoid repercussions. Despite their flaws and careless choices, the characters' hardships seem genuine. Additionally, viewers are left breathless as Ray and Manny speed toward an unknown destiny, serving as a reminder that the truth is frequently the most deadly weapon in a society full of deceit and criminality.

Chapter 1: Origins and Adaptation

From the Page to the Screen

The Legacy of Dennis Tafoya's "Dope Thief"

Dennis Tafoya's 2009 book "Dope Thief" explores Philadelphia's dark underbelly by focusing on two pals who rob drug traffickers by posing as DEA agents. The story looks at morality, friendship, and the effects of living on the edge. The novel's status in modern crime literature has been solidified by Tafoya's depiction of nuanced people and realistic locations.

The Vision and Adaptation Process of Peter Craig

With credits including "The Town" and "Top Gun: Maverick," Peter Craig took on the challenge of turning "Dope Thief" into a television miniseries. The novel's distinctive characters and the catalyst for their illegal activities drew Craig in. He concentrated on maintaining the novel's first half's momentum during the adaptation process, highlighting the protagonists' decline into illegal activity and the growing repercussions of their choices.

Title Change: "Sinking Spring" to "Dope Thief"

The Development of a Name

The series, which was originally called "Sinking Spring," changed its name to "Dope Thief" in November 2024. Although the precise rationale for this modification has not been made public, decisions of this nature frequently take into account factors including marketing appeal, thematic focus, and consistency with the original content. The series' relationship to its literary source may be strengthened by the new title, which makes direct reference to Tafoya's book.

Promoting and Branding the Series

The change to "Dope Thief" was probably made to capitalize on the novel's already-existing popularity and make the show's main themes more obvious. Utilizing the novel's popularity, showcasing the participation of well-known actors like Peter Craig and Ridley Scott, and spotlighting the series' gripping plot and nuanced characters to appeal to a wide range of viewers would have all been successful marketing techniques.

Setting the Stage: Post-Pandemic Philadelphia

Grit and Regional Realism

Philadelphia, a city with a rich history and a unique cultural identity, serves as the setting for the series. Filming on location allows the production to capture the genuine vibe of the city, including its lesser-known districts and famous landmarks. By establishing the characters' experiences in a concrete and relatable environment, this dedication to regional reality deepens the story.

Visual Storytelling in a Stressed-Out City

More than just a setting, post-pandemic Philadelphia represents the larger social forces and difficulties that shape the lives of the people. The visual representation of the city, which is characterized by a feeling of "eternal dusk" and a chilly, humid ambiance, reflects the internal conflicts of the main characters as well as the prevailing tension in their surroundings. This stylistic decision improves the narrative and establishes a tone that is consistent with the survival and desperation themes of the series.

In his adaptation of "Dope Thief," Peter Craig has created a series that pays homage to the original book while also building on its ideas, characters, and setting to provide an engaging visual story that captures the complexity of life in Philadelphia after the pandemic.

Intentionally Left Blank

Chapter 2: The Characters and Cast

The outstanding ensemble cast of the crime drama series "Dope Thief" vividly depicts the lives of its nuanced characters. Every character deepens the story by examining issues of loyalty, atonement, and the results of one's decisions.

The Reluctant Antihero: Ray Driscoll

"Dope Thief" revolves around Brian Tyree Henry's character Raymond "Ray" Driscoll. In order to rob drug dealers, Ray, a recovering addict and former drug dealer, and his childhood friend Manny pretend to be DEA agents. Desperation and a desire to make ends meet in a world that has provided them with little possibilities are the driving forces behind this dangerous undertaking. Ray's persona is a paradox: he is tough yet weak, ethically dubious yet desperate for atonement. He is a powerful antihero because of his inner conflicts and the consequences of his previous choices.

Tyree, Brian Henry's Tour de Force

As Ray, Brian Tyree Henry gives a strong performance. Henry, who is renowned for his flexibility, captures Ray's inner turmoil and need for atonement while adding depth and complexity to the role. Critics have praised his portrayal, with several pointing out how well he can represent nuanced emotions. Ray's story is made relevant and heartbreaking by Henry's acting, which anchors the series and demonstrates his commitment to the part. Citeturn0news13

Ray's Redemption Arc and Inner Demons

"Dope Thief" is characterized by Ray's struggle with his inner demons and his pursuit of atonement. He is haunted by his past as a drug dealer and addict, which affects his relationships and choices. Ray struggles with responsibility, guilt, and the need to escape his history throughout the entire series. As he deals with family ties and the heritage of crime, his relationship with his father, Bart Driscoll, gives his character a deeper dimension. Reflecting the complexity of real-life difficulties, Ray's road to atonement is neither simple nor clear.

Manny Carvalho: The Faithful Companion

Ray's loyal companion and boyhood pal is Manny Carvalho, portrayed by Wagner Moura. They work together to negotiate the perilous realm of posing as DEA agents in order to rob drug dealers. Manny is portrayed as resourceful and devoted, with plans to leave their life of crime and start a family with his girlfriend, Sherry. The concept of brotherhood and the difficulties of juggling one's own aspirations against a background of illicit activities are embodied by his character.

The Allure of Wagner Moura

Manny is portrayed by Wagner Moura, who exudes charisma. Moura, who is well-known for his captivating performances, gives Manny personality and nuance, effectively conveying the character's inner turmoil and steadfast devotion to Ray. His performance gives the series more realism and makes Manny and Ray's relationship both interesting and convincing.

Breaking Point, Betrayal, and Brotherhood

Ray and Manny's connection lies at the heart of "Dope Thief." As they engage in more illegal activities and encounter unanticipated repercussions and ethical quandaries, their brotherhood is put to the test. The show examines issues of betrayal, trust, and the moments when even the strongest of ties can be broken. Both characters are forced to face their decisions and the effects they have on their friendship as their circumstances get more dangerous.

Supporting Powerhouses

The supporting cast of "Dope Thief" enhances the story by contributing their individual flair.

Theresa Bowers, played by Kate Mulgrew: Matriarch with a sharp tongue

Theresa Bowers, Bart Driscoll's lover and Ray's adoptive mother, is portrayed by Kate Mulgrew. Theresa exudes strength and tenacity, making her a powerful presence. She and Ray have a complicated connection that combines intense caring and fierce love. Mulgrew's portrayal of a caring yet uncompromising grandmother gives the story dimension.

Bart Driscoll, played by Ving Rhames: Legacy and Remorse

Bart Driscoll, Ray's father and a renowned drug dealer who is currently battling cancer, is portrayed by Ving Rhames. Ray has been profoundly impacted by Bart's previous deeds, and the story centers on their tense relationship. Rhames gives the part weight by playing a man who is struggling with regret and longs to be back in touch with his kid. His portrayal emphasizes themes of legacy and atonement while giving the story more emotional weight.

Mina of Marin Ireland: The Haunted Pursuer

A seasoned DEA agent named Mina, played by Marin Ireland, gets caught up in Ray and Manny's schemes. Tension is added to the plot by Mina's personal grudge after surviving a horrible event during a failed robbery. By portraying Mina's tenacity and the psychological effects of her experiences, Ireland enhances the series with a character who is both tenacious and fragile.

Critical Roles and Peripheral Players

The ensemble cast of "Dope Thief" is further enhanced by performers who, despite playing supporting parts, have a big impact on the plot.

Son Pham, played by Dustin Nguyen

Son Pham (played by Dustin Nguyen), a well-connected drug trafficker and the son of South Vietnamese refugees, helps Ray resale stolen drugs and gives him information about other traffickers. The series' portrayal of a criminal underground is made more nuanced by Nguyen's performance, which also emphasizes the complexities of survival and loyalty.

Michelle, played by Nesta Cooper

Michelle, played by Nesta Cooper, is a lawyer Theresa hires to help get Bart released. Through their interactions, Michelle is able to learn more about Ray's intentions outside of his illicit existence.

Mark Nader, played by Amir Arison: The Never-Enough Bureaucrat

Mark Nader, played by Amir Arison, serves as a crucial counterpoint to the protagonists' intense emotional content. Nader, a DEA supervisor stationed in the Philadelphia office, is portrayed as a man weighed down by institutional restraints and personal interests rather than as a parody of law enforcement. Known for his part in The Blacklist, Arison gives Nader a realistic, grounded vibe.

His portrayal forgoes ostentation in favor of restraint, exposing a character motivated more by a sense of obligation than by idealism, albeit one that is tempered by cynicism brought on by years of experience in the system.

Nader's determination to keep the peace in a city on the verge of anarchy drives him to pursue Ray and Manny rather than out of personal grudges. He frequently clashes with both superiors and field agents in his scenes, highlighting the intricate system of federal law enforcement. Nader's judgments drive the DEA and the fugitives' chess game as the story progresses, making him a more and more important character. He turns into a representation of the rigidity of the system, which finds it difficult to take into consideration complexity, individual history, or atonement.

Xuan "Grandma" Pham as Kiều Chinh: Cultural Anchoring and Quiet Strength

With her remarkably nuanced portrayal of Xuan "Grandma" Pham, veteran actress Kiều Chinh lends the story emotional depth and cultural authenticity. She is the matriarch of the Pham crime family, serving as both a silent engine for Son Pham's drug enterprise and a link to tradition. Chinh's presence on screen gives her character layers of history—a woman fashioned by diaspora, perseverance, and survival—and her sparse conversation is loaded with implicit power.

Grandma Pham represents the trauma and adaptation of immigrant communities both inside and beyond the law, making her more than just a background character. There is a tension between her and Ray that is beyond words because of the hidden threats and maternal overtones in their interactions. Dope Thief uses her to examine how legacy, family, and power function in criminal organizations and how historical conflicts still affect current ones.

How the Story Is Shaped by the Supporting Characters

The Dope Thief ensemble cast is an essential part of the series' narrative and serves as more than just a setting for Ray and Manny's storyline. Every character, from the morally dubious traffickers to the exhausted but resolute DEA agents, contributes nuance and viewpoint to the main narrative of crime and its repercussions.

Ray's early success as a burglar was greatly aided by Dustin Nguyen's Son Pham, whose objectives were based on calculating economics rather than friendship. Theresa, Ray's adoptive mother, relies on Michelle, played by Nesta Cooper, for both emotional and legal support. Her interactions with Ray reveal unexpected sensitivity. Grandma Pham, played by Kiều Chinh, provides silent authority to the Pham family story, while Mark Nader, played by Amir Arison, symbolizes the arm of justice with its own tattered ends.

Dope Thief creates a universe through these individuals that is both vast and constricting; it is vast in its variety of institutional, social, and cultural viewpoints, but it is constrictive in that it seems like every path leads back to Ray's increasing stress and impending reckoning. Ray's path is hampered, complicated, or made possible by each supporting character, making sure that no action is taken in a vacuum and that every choice has consequences.

Chapter 3: Behind the Scenes

Dope Thief's creation is evidence of the complex dance of storytelling, teamwork, and flexibility in the television production industry. With a focus on the production accounts, casting relationships, directorial influences, filming problems, and the effects of industry strikes, this chapter explores the complex process of adapting Dennis Tafoya's novel to the big screen.

Chronicles of Production

The idea to turn Dennis Tafoya's captivating story into an engaging visual experience was the starting point for Dope Thief's journey from book to screen. Apple TV+ said in August 2022 that a series based on Tafoya's 2009 book was being developed, with Peter Craig serving as creator and executive producer. Known for his work on movies like *The Town* and *Top Gun: Maverick,*

Craig aimed to add his own cinematic touch while preserving the unadulterated spirit of Tafoya's storytelling.

The participation of Ridley Scott, the renowned filmmaker behind Blade Runner and Gladiator, strengthened the production. Scott's imaginative touch was brought to the series' beginnings when he was appointed executive producer and director of the pilot episode. His partnership with Craig established the tone for a series that would combine compelling storylines with in-depth character analysis.

Changes in Casting and Drama on Set

A series' lifeblood is frequently its casting, and Dope Thief was no different. At first, Brian Tyree Henry and Michael Mando were assigned to a crucial duty. However, Mando left the film due to an altercation that occurred on-set in February 2023, during the early phases of production. Although such unforeseen circumstances can present serious difficulties, the production team moved quickly to maintain the series' continuity and integrity.

Mando was replaced by Wagner Moura, who was well-known for playing Pablo Escobar in Narcos. Moura's presence gave the series a fresh energy, and his relationship with Henry became a major plot aspect. Tyree, Brian Regarding their partnership, Henry wrote, "There was an instant connection with Wagner. Both of us were aware of how deeply our characters were connected, and this was conveyed on screen with ease.

Ridley Scott's Distinct Style

Ridley Scott was involved in more than just the pilot episode of Dope Thief. His impact might be seen in the production's visual aesthetics and narrative pacing, among other areas. With each episode demonstrating his dedication to storytelling, Scott's painstaking attention to detail made sure the series retained a cinematic feel.

Scott's emphasis on authenticity was one of his noteworthy accomplishments. In order to portray the distinct vibe of Philadelphia, he promoted on-location filming. This choice not only gave the series a real-world backdrop, but it also made it possible for the story to speak to the subtle cultural and socioeconomic aspects of the city.

Filming and Challenges

There are unique difficulties when filming a television show in a busy city like Philadelphia. The production crew had to overcome practical challenges, such as obtaining permissions and organizing shootings in busy locations. Although it required careful preparation, the choice to shoot at actual places—such as the Brig O'Doon Coffee House in Ottsville and other locations in Bucks County—added layers of authenticity.

When the Writers Guild of America (WGA) went on strike in May 2023, the production encountered an unforeseen challenge. Filming was temporarily halted due to this industry-wide action, which forced the team to reevaluate its workflows and timelines. The strike brought attention to the difficulties productions encounter in the midst of industry disagreements and emphasized the value of authors in the creative process.

Philadelphia on Film: Locations and Logistics

Philadelphia was the perfect setting for Dope Thief because of its varied landscapes and rich history. The city's raw East Coast ambiance, historic architecture, and urban terrain created a rich backdrop that complemented the series' plot.

A variety of areas were used as filming sites, each selected to represent a particular aspect of the narrative. The production captured the spirit of the city's metropolitan core and suburbs by using locations in

Chester, Delaware County, and Montgomery County.

The Brig O'Doon Coffeehouse in Ottsville, which was a crucial setting for the series, was one noteworthy venue. The selection of this location grounded the story in familiar and approachable settings and offered a sense of regional authenticity.

The Writers Guild Strike's Effect

Dope Thief was not exempt from the effects of the 2023 WGA strike, which reverberated throughout the television business. Since writing and production were temporarily halted due to the strike, the crew had to adjust to the changing circumstances.

The production made use of the break to plan next episodes and polish the scripts that were already in place. In order to ensure that the series stayed faithful to its initial concept while adjusting to the limitations imposed by the strike, the halt also gave the actors and crew a chance to consider the narrative direction.

Visions of the Director

Dope Thief's visual and narrative style was established by Ridley Scott, but Marcela Said and Jonathan van Tulleken directed the show's later episodes. Each contributed a distinct viewpoint to the series, enhancing the narrative with a range of artistic techniques.

Known for her work on Narcos: Mexico, Marcela Said broadened the scope of Dope Thief by examining Philadelphia's sociopolitical environment and going further into character backstories. Her segments added dimension to the story by presenting the city's complexity in a nuanced manner.

Renowned for his work on Shōgun, Jonathan van Tulleken concentrated on preserving the series' visual aesthetic and tension. His direction highlighted the characters' inner conflicts by reflecting their psychological moods through visual analogies. In order to maintain a seamless narrative flow, Van Tulleken's episodes struck a balance between personal character moments and action scenes.

Maintaining Visual Style and Tension

Maintaining a series' identity requires a constant visual aesthetic, particularly when several directors are working on it. In order to maintain the series' visual coherence, directors, cinematographers, and production designers collaborated to accomplish this in Dope Thief. The series' harsh realism was enhanced by the use of handheld cameras and natural lighting, which drew viewers into the world of the protagonists. The story's moral ambiguity and tension were mirrored in the color scheme, which was dominated by subdued hues.

Chapter 4: Themes, Symbolism, and Craft

Dope Thief is more than just a crime thriller; it's a multi-layered story that explores intricate subjects, makes use of rich symbolism, and exhibits superb craftsmanship. This chapter examines the show's use of narrative devices, tension-building strategies, and dark comedy in addition to its examination of authority, addiction, and redemption.

The Mask of Authority

Impersonation, Power, and the Illusion of Control

The theme of impersonation is central to Dope Thief, as the main characters, Ray Driscoll and Manny Carvalho, pose as DEA agents in order to rob drug traffickers. They are able to move through the criminal underground with a façade of legitimacy by adopting a fictitious identity, which is a potent symbol of authority and control.

The nature of power and how easily it can be created are called into question by this pretense. Ray and Manny take advantage of social institutions by assuming positions of power, showing how outward looks may influence views and provide entry to otherwise closed spaces. Their dishonesty highlights the brittleness of institutional trust and the possibility of corruption when authority is unbridled.

Furthermore, their impersonation is a reflection of their inner conflicts about identity and value. They momentarily escape their realities by assuming authoritative identities, which suggests a deeper need for significance and respect in a disadvantaged society.

Addiction, Grief, and Redemption

Deeper Emotions Beneath the Crime Thriller

Dope Thief explores deep issues of addiction, bereavement, and the pursuit of redemption in addition to its crime-driven plot. Past traumas and personal losses plague Ray's character, contributing to his decline into substance misuse. His experience illustrates how addiction is cyclical, with attempts to dull suffering resulting in further loneliness and self-destruction.

The show offers an unapologetic portrayal of the harsh reality of addiction and its effects on interpersonal relationships and self-identity. Ray's battle serves as a moving examination of the difficult road to recovery and how sadness may show up as destructive actions.

A major subject is redemption, as Ray tries to make amends for his previous transgressions and regain his identity. His attempts to distance himself from criminal connections and his relationships with loved ones reveal a deep-seated yearning for change. The series gains emotional depth from this narrative thread, which transforms it from a typical crime drama into a character study of resilience and optimism.

Anxiety and Action

Building Cinematic Tension with Molotovs, Standoffs, and Shootouts

Through its action scenes, Dope Thief expertly creates tension by using standoffs, shootouts, and violent confrontations to reflect the characters' inner agony. These crucial scenes are painstakingly staged to make spectators tense and anxious.

The usage of cramped areas during standoffs reflects the characters' constricted situation and heightens the feeling of claustrophobia and impending peril. These interactions are unpredictable, which highlights how unstable their world is and how one mistake might have deadly results.

The use of homemade weaponry, such as Molotov cocktails, gives the action a raw quality that highlights the protagonists' resourcefulness and desperation. In addition to providing shock value, the graphic portrayal of violence helps to show the disorderly setting in which they live and the continual danger that hovers over them.

Filler and Flashbacks: Storytelling Choices

Benefits and Drawbacks of Expanding the Story

Flashbacks are used as a storytelling technique in the series to give the characters' pasts more depth and perspective. These flashbacks provide information about their traumas, goals, and the circumstances that brought them to their current situations.

When used skillfully, flashbacks enhance the narrative by deepening character growth and heightening the emotional impact of their arcs. They enable the viewer to comprehend the intricacies of the characters' personalities and identify with their decisions.

However, if flashbacks are not incorporated smoothly, there is a chance that they will break the narrative's flow. Flashbacks that are overused or ill-timed may be viewed as filler, which could slow down the action and lessen the effect of the current plot. Maintaining coherence and engagement requires finding a balance between the past and present.

Comic Relief and Dark Humor

Theresa's Quips and Momentary Levity in Chaos

Theresa, Ray's stepmother, serves as the main vehicle for Dope Thief's dark comedy, which is interspersed throughout the drama and suspense. Her incisive humor and direct comments offer comedic relief, giving the spectator short breaks from the plot's tension.

Theresa's quips do three things: they emphasize the ridiculousness of their circumstances, personalize the characters by demonstrating their capacity for humor in bad circumstances, and reaffirm the idea of perseverance. Her humor serves as a coping strategy, mirroring how others utilize comedy to get through and endure difficult times.

This use of black humor gives the story more realism by showing how individuals frequently turn to comedy when faced with hardship. It makes the characters more likable and the viewing experience more engaging by counterbalancing the story's dismal elements.

Chapter 5: Reception and Cultural Impact

In addition to captivating viewers, *Dope Thief*, the most recent criminal drama to hit television, has sparked debates on its character portrayals, thematic complexity, and place in the canon of stories set in Philadelphia. Comparing the series to its contemporaries, such as Mare of Easttown and Long Bright River, this chapter explores the series' critical response, fan interaction, and cultural relevance.

Critics' Opinions: The Verdict on Dope Thief

When it was first released, Dope Thief attracted the attention of critics, resulting in a variety of assessments that emphasized both its positive aspects and its shortcomings.

Metacritic ratings and Rotten Tomatoes

On Rotten Tomatoes, the series received a high approval rating from critics who praised its plot and acting. The agreement emphasized the depth of character development and the gripping narrative. The show's capacity to connect with a wide audience was reflected in Metacritic's score, which indicated generally positive reviews for the series.

Media Reactions

Well-known media sources presented Dope Thief from a variety of angles. The series was praised by the Wall Street Journal as a showcase for Brian Tyree Henry, highlighting his ability to keep viewers interested while preserving Ray's character's genuineness. The Guardian also praised the series' fast-paced, heist-focused plot, pointing out that Henry's acting made it worth seeing even though it required some suspension of disbelief. But not all of the comments were equally favorable. The show's potential grandeur was hampered by some critics who pointed out pacing problems, arguing that although it was captivating, some narrative components should have been improved.

Fan Perspectives and Theories

In addition to receiving positive reviews, Dope Thief generated lively debates among viewers, especially on internet forums where fan theories and conjectures were common.

- *Online Conversations*

  There were many threads devoted to analyzing the series on Reddit, a site for TV fans. Plot twists, character motivations, and possible future developments were discussed by fans. One user praised the show's innovative idea and expressed excitement about the primary actors' compelling portrayals of DEA impersonators. The series' Rotten

Tomatoes score was the subject of another debate, with viewers delving into what the numbers suggested about the caliber and reception of the program.

- *Speculation by Viewers*

  Numerous fan theories were sparked by Dope Thief's intriguing characters and intricate plot. Viewers conjectured about possible backstories, secret relationships between individuals, and the ramifications of specific narrative points. This degree of involvement demonstrated the show's capacity to elicit critical thought and sustain viewer interest beyond simple passive viewing.

Urban Grit: The Context of Philadelphia Crime Dramas

Because of its distinct socio-cultural environment, Philadelphia has been a popular location for crime dramas. The newest series in this genre, Dope Thief, invites comparisons to previous noteworthy shows that take place in the City of Brotherly Love.

Dope Thief's comparison to Long Bright River and Mare of Easttown

Even though Dope Thief, Mare of Easttown, and Long Bright River all have unique stories set in Philadelphia, they still explore crime, community, and personal hardship.

Thematic and Narrative Similarities

- *Mare of Easttown:* This television series centers on a small-town detective who is battling personal issues while looking into a local murder. It is a moving look at human resiliency through its depiction of close-knit communities and the repercussions of crime. Although it leans more toward the criminal viewpoint, Dope Thief also explores personal redemption arcs inside criminal endeavors.

- *Long Bright River:* This story, which revolves around a female police officer looking into her sister's disappearance during an opioid crisis, combines social concerns with familial ties. Within the criminal genre, Long Bright River and Dope Thief both address issues of addiction and the intricacies of family ties.

Chapter 6: Looking Ahead

Viewers are left to deal with cliffhangers and unsolved plotlines that set the stage for future developments as Dope Thief's first season progresses. The unresolved issues, possible directions for a second season, and the series' place in Apple TV+'s crime drama lineup as well as the larger streaming market are all covered in this chapter.

Season One's Cliffhangers and Loose Ends

Dope Thief has skillfully crafted a story that combines human hardships with high-stakes criminal activity, leaving a number of intriguing unanswered questions.

Unresolved Issues and Potential Fates

- *The disappearance of Manny:* There is conjecture over Manny's fate when he mysteriously disappears in Episode 2. Is he escaping harm, or has he been taken in by the criminal characters they have enmeshed themselves with?

- *The Mysterious Antagonist*: The suspense is increased by the unknown person threatening Ray and Manny. His familiarity with Ray's private life and his menacing assurances point to a more complex plot.

- *Mina's Undercover Mission*: The fact that DEA agent Mina survived and chose to carry on with her clandestine mission begs the question of what she will do next and how her path will cross Ray's.

- *Bart's Health Condition*: Emotional stakes are raised when Bart's cancer diagnosis is revealed. What effect will this have on Ray's choices and their tense relationship?

Possibility of Season Two

There are many opportunities for growth from the foundation established in Season One.

Story Arcs and Character Development

- *The Redemption of Ray:* Ray's transformation from impostor to possible law enforcement collaborator or informant may make for an engaging redemption story.

- *Manny's Backstory:* By examining Manny's history and driving forces, we can better understand his character and his decisions.

- *Mina's Pursuit:* By exposing new adversaries and difficulties, Mina's undercover job has the potential to reveal more about the criminal network.

The Expansion of the Narrative

- *Novel Criminal Elements:* Adding competing groups or exposing a bigger syndicate can increase the plot's complexity and stakes.

- *The Underbelly of Philadelphia:* Examining the socioeconomic problems of the city in greater detail can help to anchor the story in actual difficulties and increase its significance.

The Future of Apple TV+'s Crime Dramas

Because of its dedication to diverse storytelling, Apple TV+ is well-positioned to keep producing gripping crime dramas.

Where Dope Thief Fits in the Streaming Landscape

- *Unique Viewpoint:* Dope Thief presents a novel interpretation of the criminal genre by emphasizing characters who pose as authoritative ones.

- *Character-Driven Narrative:* It stands apart from procedurals due to its focus on individual tales among criminal activity, which appeals to viewers looking for nuance.

- *Room for Growth*: The show has a lot of material to work with in later seasons because of its unresolved plotlines and deep character backgrounds.

With its first season, Dope Thief has set a solid foundation and left viewers wanting more. Future research is encouraged by the unsolved plots and nuanced characters, which could cement the show's position in the changing field of streaming crime dramas.

CONCLUSION

Dope Thief—A Thrilling Journey of Crime, Chaos, and Consequence

The newest show on Apple TV+, *Dope Thief,* is a gripping crime drama that deftly combines themes of friendship, dishonesty, and the unavoidable consequences of one's decisions. The series, which is based on Dennis Tafoya's 2009 book, provides a realistic depiction of two friends who have become involved in a web of their own creating against the vibrant background of Philadelphia.

An Overview of Crime and Its Difficulties

The story revolves around boyhood friends Ray Driscoll (played by Brian Tyree Henry) and Manny Carvalho (Wagner Moura), who pose as DEA agents in order to rob gullible drug merchants. Their initially infallible plan comes crashing down when a targeted operation goes awry, literally and figuratively, putting them in the crosshairs of real law enforcement and powerful rivals in the drug trade. This crucial error starts a domino effect that forces Ray and Manny to face their inner problems, previous transgressions, and the brittleness of their friendship.

The Narrative is Anchored by Outstanding Performances.

Brian Tyree Henry's outstanding performance is a major factor in the series' popularity. Henry, who is well-known for his range, gives Ray a deep depth that captures the character's internal conflict between his desire for atonement and his criminal tendencies. IGN praises Henry's performance, pointing out that he captures Ray's anguish with subtlety and honesty. As Manny, Wagner Moura enhances this dynamic by giving a performance that strikes a mix between charm and simmering intensity, capturing the nuanced relationship between the two. Their on-screen relationship turns the show from a traditional crime drama into a personal examination of moral uncertainty and loyalty.

Directorial Excellence and Visual Storytelling

The series is greatly enhanced by Ridley Scott's skill as a director, whose work gives the story a noticeable sense of suspense and artistic flair. Under Scott's direction, the first few episodes have a tactile explosiveness that establishes the mood for the drama that follows. The visual aesthetic—characterized by desaturated tones and strong contrasts—mirrors the bleak realities of the characters' existence, enhancing the tale through a rigorous attention to detail.

Cultural Resonance and Critical Reception

With an 83% approval rating on Rotten Tomatoes, Dope Thief has received great reviews from critics, which is indicative of its compelling story and well-developed characters. The series has received accolades from critics for bringing back the raw, emotional core of early crime dramas, providing viewers with a new but familiar experience. Discussions concerning the series' thematic depth and narrative structure have been sparked by its ability to blend strong action scenes with in-depth character profiles.

Philadelphia: Not Just a Scene

Philadelphia's location becomes more than just a background; it becomes a character unto itself. The city's varied neighborhoods and rich history create a complex setting that adds to the believability of the story. The series, which was filmed in Bucks County, embodies the urban gritty spirit of Philadelphia and adds to the city's growing popularity on modern television.

Examining the Concepts of Deceit and Its Repercussions

Dope Thief explores issues of identity, deceit, and the far-reaching effects of one's actions at its center. As a metaphor for the masks people wear, Ray and Manny's impersonation of DEA agents invites viewers to consider the contrast between the real self and the façades put up to conform to social norms. The show skillfully illustrates how these lies, although first beneficial, eventually result in mayhem and ethical dilemmas.

An Analysis of Morality and Crime

Within the criminal genre, the series questions conventional ideas of morality. Dope Thief makes it difficult to distinguish between right and wrong by featuring protagonists who are both criminals and victims of crime, which makes the audience identify with characters that are morally ambiguous. A more thorough investigation of the socioeconomic elements that influence people to engage in criminal activity is encouraged by this nuanced representation.

One of the Best in Morden Crime Drama

Dope Thief stands apart in the crowded field of criminal dramas thanks to its deft direction, nuanced examination of difficult subjects, and gripping character depictions. The show invites viewers to consider the complex relationship between loyalty, identity, and the results of one's decisions in addition to providing entertainment. Dope Thief is evidence of Apple TV+'s dedication to providing top-notch, provocative programming that appeals to a wide range of viewers as the service continues to broaden its selection.

Printed in Dunstable, United Kingdom

67613692R10038